FAMILY V̶

around

CARDIFF & THE VALLEYS

Gordon Hindess

Scarthin Books, Cromford, Derbyshire 1992

FAMILY WALKS
AROUND
CARDIFF AND THE VALLEYS

Family Walks Series
General Editor: Norman Taylor

THE COUNTRY CODE

Guard against all risk of fire
Fasten all gates
Keep dogs under proper control
Keep to paths across farmland
Avoid damaging fences, hedges and walls
Leave no litter
Safeguard water supplies
Protect wildlife,wild plants and trees
Go carefully along country roads
Respect the life of the countryside

Published by Scarthin Books, Cromford, Derbyshire

Phototypesetting, printing by Nuffield Press Ltd., Cowley, Oxford.

ISBN 0 907758 54 1

WOODLAND PATH (Route 14)

1

Preface

Mid and South Glamorgan are largely undiscovered by walkers, who head instead for the Brecon Beacons, Pembrokeshire or the Wye Valley and Forest of Dean. But the industrial heart of South Wales has much to offer: it has mountains, valleys, lowland hills, coast and forests in close proximity and of a quality to rival any of the traditional tourist areas. A glance at a road atlas may be a deterrent, with development and roads shown at an exaggerated scale and leaving little room for 'green' in between. The density of development and industrialisation cannot be denied and not all of it is pleasing to the eye. But the power of nature still dwarfs the blunderings of man: the underlying geology, shaped by glaciation and erosion with great character, provides a variety of soils and habitats that guarantees a wide range of flora and fauna. There are walks here to suit all tastes—but do not take my word for it, come and see for yourself.

Dedication

This book is dedicated to the memory of Len Goddon, always a countryman at heart and the ideal companion on a family walk.

Acknowledgement

To Liz, Clare, Mark and Paul for allowing me time off from the family to write this book.

About the Author

Gordon Hindess is married and his three children have grown up in Cardiff, so this volume includes some of his own 'family walks'. Gordon is a chartered civil engineer for whom walking is the mental and physical therapy that counters the pressures of the working week. An interest in nature has been supplemented by an active study of the industrial archaeology and geology of South Wales. For some years, he has planned or led hikes in the area for the local cubs, scouts, guides and ventures, but he felt that it was now time to introduce the pleasures of the countryside around Cardiff and the Valleys to a wider audience.

CONTENTS

LOCATION MAP

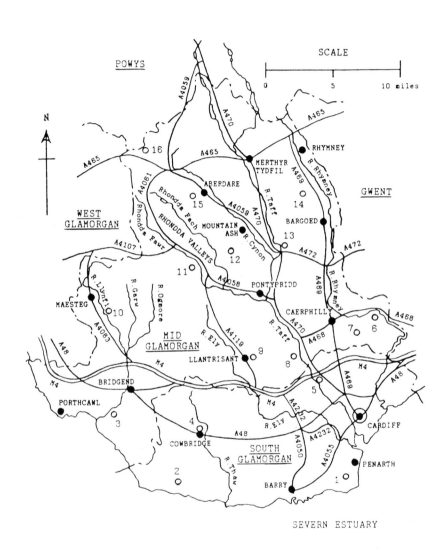

4

Introduction

For the purpose of this book of walks around Cardiff and the Valleys, routes have been chosen in the counties of Mid and South Glamorgan. The former, occupying the centre of the South Wales coalfield, is an area of deep valleys cut into a sandstone plateau, which rises from a general level of about 800 feet above sea level in the south to almost 2000 feet at its highest in the north. South Glamorgan encompasses Cardiff itself and the rolling, mainly limestone, hills of the Vale of Glamorgan, a district that remains predominantly rural in nature. Whether you are looking for the undemanding enjoyment of the countryside and pleasant views or the more detailed study of birds, plants, geology or industrial archaeology, you will find something of interest here.

Do not be deterred by an out-of-date and false vision of a grimy, over-exploited and scarred country. The decline of the traditional heavy industries, the closure of many railway lines and the spur given to reclamation by the Aberfan disaster in 1966 have done much to correct 100 years or more of neglect and putting the environment second to profit. The once polluted river is being fished: reservoirs and quarries are lakes at the heart of country parks: the functional viaduct may be crumbling a little, but it has mellowed and blended into the landscape as a graceful feature: and the disused railway, tramroad or canal is a linear nature reserve, a haven for plants and animals . . . and a walking route with the gentlest of gradients.

For children, a walk should be a mixture of fun and exploration—an adventure or an expedition. Get them involved seeking items of interest and route finding: if the directions say 'look for a stile on the left', let them discover it. Encourage their curiosity and take time to answer their questions, even if its means carrying a pocket guide to flowers, birds or whatever. Remember, too, that a family does not have to be restricted to two generations: grandparents and grandchildren often find a close affinity in the countryside and granny or grandad often turns out to be a walking encyclopaedia of natural history.

The theme of a walk will depend on the interests of the party, the ages of children, the weather and the season, but the ingredients to suit all tastes and conditions abound in this book.

Choosing a walk

If you walk regularly, you will have a good idea of your family's capability and should find it easy to select suitable routes from the Appendix which ranks them in order of difficulty. If you are not sure, then always go for a less strenuous option. The severity of a walk is a subjective assessment which takes account of length, amount of climbing (and its steepness and distribution) and the conditions of paths. It is difficult to avoid hills in South Wales, so nearly all routes have some climbing. Do not be put off by this: just remember to take ascents at a comfortable speed with plenty of stops to enjoy the scenery. In most of the walks, a shorter variation is described so, if the going proves tougher than expected or the weather deteriorates, the trip can be curtailed without the frustration of retracing one's steps.

Timing

Allow time for the slowest member of the party not to feel rushed. With younger children, a mile an hour may be a realistic speed: by the time they are 10, 2 miles an hour may be achieved—but be sure to allow time for play, exploration and a lunch stop. Teenage children may need to accept that their parents' speed is the governing factor!

Clothing

Sensible footwear is of prime importance. Regular walkers will undoubtedly go for proper boots but, in most cases, stout comfortable shoes will suffice and trainers may be preferred in dry conditions. Children may be happy in wellies, especially those who would rate a muddy section as the highlight of the route. Comfort and a good grip are more important than expensive boots that will be too small in six months' time. Remember that the weather can be deceptive and can change in an hour or two—be prepared with jumpers and waterproofs, with the emphasis on layers of clothing to enable the optimum comfort level to be maintained, and take woolly hats and gloves in your rucksack, even if it seems warm enough at the start: there can be a world of difference between a sheltered valley and an exposed ridge.

Other Equipment

If you walk regularly, a rucksack is essential: it is by far the easiest way to carry things and leaves hands free for gates, stiles . . . and children! What goes in it? Waterproofs and spare clothing to start, then lunch if a picnic is planned. Even if not, it is a good idea to carry chocolate bars or other high

6

calorie 'emergency' rations and a drink (hot in winter). Binoculars are very handy for identifying birds and distant features and a camera will record the highlights of a walk. While the sketch maps and route descriptions should prove more than adequate for navigation, many walkers will want to carry the local Ordnance Survey map (Landranger sheet references are given for each route) and, possibly, a compass. There are many good pocket guides on natural history to take as an aid to field identification. Finally, a small first aid kit is a good idea—children can be remarkably adept at falling over or getting stung.

Paths

In the main, routes use public footpaths, with a few permissive paths and waymarked trails in Forestry Commission land, nature reserves and public parkland. Where roads are unavoidable, they are generally very quiet or, in the few cases where they are busy, have footpaths or good verges beside them.

Refreshments

Nearly all of the walks have convenient pubs, teashops, etc., on route. If they do not, suggestions for obtaining sustenance close by are made. Most pubs cater for children, although the only acceptable facilities may be outside tables. Muddy boots may not be welcome and it is polite to check with the proprietor before consuming your own food in his premises. There are official picnic sites on many of the routes or you may prefer to choose a convenient sheltered corner or viewpoint elsewhere . . . remembering, of course, to take your litter home with you.

Public Transport

The starting point for most walks is on or close to a bus route, while some of the routes can also be reached by train. There has been intense competition between bus companies in recent years with consequential changes to routes, timetables and operators. It is, therefore, advisable to check with companies in advance, particularly in the more remote locations. Public transport details, at the time of preparation of the walks, are given for each route, with bus company and British Rail particulars in the Appendix.

Symbols used on the route maps

— — ➔ —	Route on path or unsurfaced track
═══════	Metalled road or track
➔	Direction of route on above
• • • • •	Path or track *not* on route
┼┼┼┼┼○┼┼┼	Railway and station
～～～～	Large river or canal
～～～～	Small river or stream
(trees)	Coniferous/deciduous woodland
+ ▪	Church/building mentioned in text
④ etc.	Number corresponds with route description
⌒⌒⌒⌒⌒	Crag or quarry
⌒⌒⌒	Coastal cliff
• 231	Spot height in metres above sea level (100 metres = 328 feet)
P	Car park (all free when walks compiled)

8

Route 1   3½ miles
Cosmeston and Lavernock

Outline   Cosmeston — St. Mary's Well Bay — Lavernock Point — Penarth — Cosmeston.

Summary   Stroll through the Country Park then across to the coast for a fossil-hunting exploration of the foreshore and a walk along the cliff top path, with its views across the Bristol Channel. Only gentle hills are encountered on the way, but allow plenty of time for children who may want to linger on the beach or at the adventure playground in the Park.

Attractions   Cosmeston Lakes Country Park shows what can be achieved from the unpromising starting point of an old limestone quarry, once used as a refuse tip. It now offers walking, riding and conservation areas with facilities for watersports, picnics and barbecues. Children will enjoy the Adventure Playground, while the heritage project, involving the excavation and reconstruction of a medieval village, is quite unique in Britain.
   Lavernock Point marks the end of one of the most ambitious of the Severn Barrage proposals and provides an excellent vantage point to view the projected line, via the islands of Flat Holm and Steep Holm, to Brean Down, near Weston-Super-Mare. It was here, on this same line, that Marconi first communicated across water by radio in May 1897. Looking west along the coast, the smaller Sully Island can be seen. If you have time and the tide is out, it is possible to cross over on a natural causeway formed at a geological fault: the round trip from St. Mary's Well Bay would add about two miles to the walk.
   The traverse of the foreshore from St. Mary's Well Bay to Lavernock Point should only be attempted when the tide is falling or well out. It is worth reminding visitors to the area that the estuary enjoys one of the highest tidal ranges in the world—but it does not take any longer to come in! With small children, allow at least an hour for this section. While there are sandy areas, the main feature of the shore is the gently dished limestone terracing. Some of these layers of rock are full of fossils—ammonites, bivalves (like scallops of today) and brachiopods—but they are not often clearly exposed on the upper surface. Look out for loose, freshly broken cobbles for the best examples, especially as the Point is approached.

Refreshments   The route passes the Golden Hind and Schooner inns, while the visitor centre in the park has a small cafe. But you may prefer to picnic or have a barbecue (the hired ranges need to be booked in advance) in the Country Park.

9

Route 1
Cosmeston and Lavernock

3½ miles

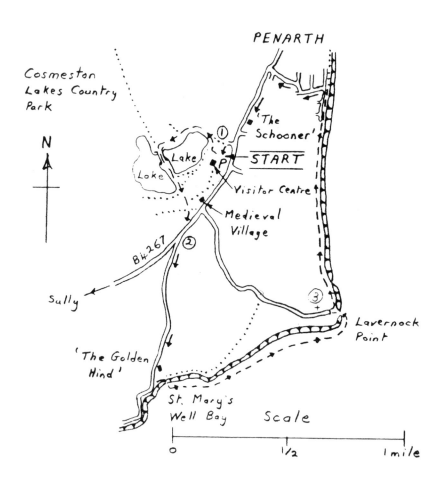

Route 1
Cosmeston and Lavernock   3½ miles

START: *Car park in Cosmeston Lakes Country Park, off the B4267 (O.S. Sheet 171 G.R. 179 692)*

ROUTE

1. *Leave the car park and skirt the nearer watersports lake in an anticlockwise direction until you meet the main north-west–south-east path just north of the bridge over the channel between the two lakes. Go left across the bridge and keep straight on, beyond the lakes and passing the medieval village on your left, until the main road is reached. Go straight across.*

2. *Take the minor road to St. Mary's Well Bay, passing under the disused railway bridge and by the caravan park entrance, The Golden Hind and a car park all on the left. Just past the car park, take the footpath on the left. After 100 yards, go down the path to the beach. (If the tide is in or the foreshore does not appeal, continue on the cliff-top path until this meets a road, where a right turn will take you to 3.) Head left across the beach and rocks to Lavernock Point. 50 yards after rounding the Point, go up the rough steps and along the short track to the end of the road. Turn sharply to the right.*

3. *Follow the coastal path until it becomes surfaced in a wide verge opposite the first houses of Penarth. Take the third road (Stanton Way) on the left. Where this becomes Halton Close, go right and then left over the bridge over the disused railway and continue to the main road. Head left, passing The Schooner, before crossing the road to return to the Country Park.*

ACCESS BY BUS
Welsh National Bustler services P4, P5 and P8 stop frequently at the entrance to the Park.

TRESILIAN BAY

Refreshments   There are a number of hospitable pubs and other eating places in Llantwit Major and a cafe at Col-huw Beach. Snacks can be obtained at the car park at Nash Point in the summer, while the Horseshoe Inn at Marcross is conveniently close to the bus stop.

12

Route 2

3½ miles
(linear variation of 5½ miles)

Llantwit Major

Outline Llantwit Major — Cwm Col-huw — Tresilian Bay — Llantwit Major.

Summary This is a relatively easy walk with only a few short climbs. The route takes in meadowland, a nature reserve and part of the coastal path, offering views of the local cliffs and the English coastline.

Those who enjoy flowers will find the walk particularly rewarding. As a variation, a longer linear walk, past a castle and a lighthouse, can be undertaken from Marcross, a short bus ride from Llantwit Major.

Attractions The narrow streets of Llantwit Major contain buildings dating back to the 13th century. The Town Hall has external steps for the town crier, while the church is noted for its painted wall frescoes and font, crosses and carved pillars more than 1000 years old. You cannot miss the dovecote, but can you find the medieval gatehouse with its present front door at first floor level?

The steep sides of Cwm Col-huw (or Colhugh) are covered by bushes and trees, the hawthorn blossom whitening the valley in May. The route passes through the Nature Reserve on the side of the valley and Castle Ditches, the remains of a Celtic Hillfort. Col-huw Beach is mainly rocky, but some sand is exposed at low tide. The fossil Gryphaea, or Devil's Toenail, may be found though generally well embedded in the surrounding rock. The limestone here is well jointed (vertical cracks), has nearly horizontal bedding and alternates with thin shaley bands. This combination is responsible for the sheer cliffs, like the walls of a giant's castle, and the rock platforms of the foreshore. It also makes the cliffs extremely unstable and the warning signs along the coast should not be ignored.

A wide range of flowers can be found in conditions ranging from pasture to exposed cliff top to shaded woodland to stream bank. Look out for kidney vetch, gromwell and wild chive.

The longer variation from Marcross takes you by St. Donat's Castle and Nash Point Lighthouse. The 14th century castle was restored earlier this century and is now the home of Atlantic College. The lighthouse is open to visitors occasionally: a telephone call in advance (0446 793471) is advised to avoid disappointment. It is worth finding out about the fog-horn, the second (now disused) lighthouse and the colour-coded flashes of today.

continued opposite

13

Route 2
Llantwit Major

3½ miles

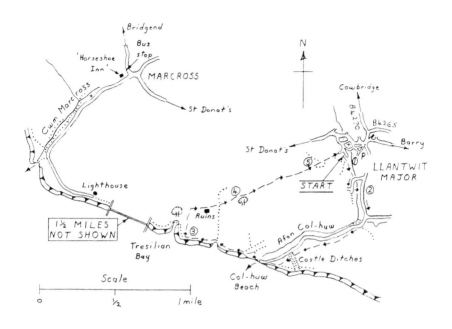

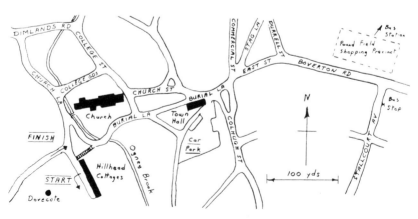

Route 2
Llantwit Major

3½ miles
(linear variation of 5½ miles)

START: *Car park immediately behind the Town Hall (O.S. Sheet 170 G.R. 967 687). The route description starts at Hillhead Cottages (see detailed street plan).*

ROUTE

1. *Enter the field via the stone steps and stile near the dovecote. Turn left and walk to the south-east corner of the field, cross the stile and follow the path down some steps into the farm yard. Keep straight on and, at the road, go right. Just after passing 'Colhugh Park' on your right, take the narrow path on the left, cross the stream on a footbridge and emerge carefully on to the road. Turn right.*

2. *Follow the road for ¼ mile, passing 'Millay Lane' on your left. Where a farm access joins the road from the left, enter Cwm Colhugh Nature Reserve via the stone stile straight ahead. The path rises to the top of the valley side, goes through a kissing gate and on, through Castle Ditches, to join the coastal path. Go right here and follow the zig-zag path down to the small car park. Pass to the left of, then immediately behind, the beach cafe and shop. Go up the steps on the left, taking the coastal path to the cliff top, and turn left. Follow the coastal path for nearly ½ mile, ignoring one path to the right at a small rocky inlet.*

3. *Just before Tresilian Bay, go over the stile in the stone wall on your right. The path runs between a fence and wall until it crosses a stile and then keeps the wall on its right until some steps allow it to pass through the wall. Cross the field, passing just to the left of the ruined buildings. Immediately after crossing the Dimhole—St. Donats path (marked by a stone plaque), go over the stone stile and cross the field, heading for the left side of a copse. At the corner of the copse, go over the stone stile on your left and turn right.*

4. *Follow the edge of the copse to its north-east corner, bear slightly left and head across the field for the corner of a hedged field. At this corner, go over the stile and follow the right hand field boundary. Two more stone stiles take you quickly in and out of a small field. Bear right to cross the next field, heading for another stone stile. Over this stile, keep the field boundary on your left and cross to the next field via a stone stile. Bear slightly right and head for the short section of wall in the opposite boundary.*

15

5. *Go over the stile to the left of the wall, then, keeping the field boundary on your right, go over two more stiles to join a track. Go straight on: the track improves to become a surfaced road which ends at the T-junction just north of Hillhead Cottages.*

Variation

Catch the bus to Marcross from the Bus Station or Stallcourt Avenue (see street plan). Take the road to the beach and, just before the red 'warning' sign, enter the nature reserve on the right. Take either of the two paths through the reserve to emerge in a steep-sided grassy valley. Take the track which climbs the left side to join the road by the refreshment kiosk. Follow the road to Nash Point lighthouse then continue on the coastal path, crossing the massive sea wall at St. Donat's Castle (about 1 mile) and Tresilian Bay (a further mile). Just past this bay, join the circular route at 3, the stile now being on your left.

ACCESS BY BUS

Llantwit Major is well served by National Welsh buses. The Bustler service V3 to Marcross is 2–3 hourly: it is advisable to check times if doing the longer walk.

OGMORE CASTLE

Route 3

3 miles
(shorter variation 1½ miles)

Ogmore and Merthyr Mawr

Outline Ogmore Castle — Merthyr Mawr — Candleston Castle — Merthyr Mawr — Ogmore Castle.

Summary A short walk with very little climbing—but packed with interesting things: two ruined castles, a picturesque village with thatched cottages and the stepping stones across the River Ewenny. The route crosses water-meadows and farmland, and skirts the sand-dunes of Merthyr Mawr Warren, while never being far from woodland at any time, so a wide variety of flora and fauna can be expected.

Attractions The 12th century Ogmore Castle may be a ruin, but it is in a near perfect setting beside the River Ewenny, where it guarded an important river crossing—still marked by stepping stones. These stones will appeal to children, especially if Mum or Dad manages to fall in the river: so take care if the stones are wet. A few of the very highest tides of the year cover the stones—but only for a short period. If you meet this situation, follow the last ½ mile of the route (which uses the footbridge just upstream) first: the stones will be clear on your return.

Merthyr Mawr is an unspoilt village with scattered cottages, most of which are thatched. St. Teilo's Church, rebuilt in the last century, is worth a visit. Candleston Castle, a fortified manor house dating from the 14th century, is now an ivy covered ruin, but a picturesque setting for the adjacent picnic area. The extensive sand dunes of Merthyr Mawr Warren overlie a limestone hill, making them reputedly the highest dune system in Britain. The Warren is a Site of Special Scientific Interest and can be explored from a number of points on the route—but do not let small children wander off into the dunes alone as they could easily get lost. The area offers a wide range of plants: look out for Wild Thyme, Viper's Bugloss and Yellow Stonecrop.

Only a mile from Ogmore Castle is Ogmore-by-Sea, where children may enjoy the sandy beach or a clamber over the rocks. The rocks display an extensive range of fossils, including corals and crinoids (a relative of today's sea urchin). Perhaps the easiest to find is the single coral Syphonophillia, looking like a petrified banana skin. For more serious geologists, an unconformity (a gap in the geological sequence) and breccia filled valleys can be found.

Refreshments Farmhouse teas are available at Ogmore Farm and snacks and ice cream at Ton Farm. The Pelican offers a range of snacks and meals or you may picnic at either of the castles.

Route 3
Ogmore and Merthyr Mawr

3 miles

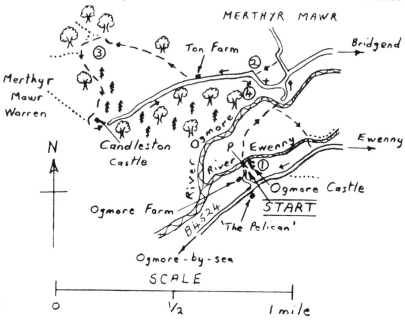

COTTAGE, MERTHYR MAWR

Route 3
Ogmore and Merthyr Mawr
3 miles
(shorter variation of 1½ miles)

START: *Car park adjacent to Ogmore Castle, which is beside the B4524 (O.S. Sheet 170 G.R. 882 769).*

ROUTE:

1. *Cross the River Ewenny on the stepping stones and continue on the path ahead with a wall on your right. At the River Ogmore, cross the footbridge and follow the road into Merthyr Mawr. Go right at the T-junction and then take the first road on the left. After 100 yards, go over the stone stile on the left which is to the right of a gate, and head straight across the field. Go through a gate into a rough woodland and follow the track until it emerges via a gate on to the road.*

2. *Go straight ahead on the road. Immediately after Ton Farm go over the stile on the right (a plaque at the stile is signed to Tythegston and Newton). Go up the hill, heading for the left end of a wood with the field boundary on your right. At the top of the field, cross the stone stile (why does it remind you of a Polo?) and continue uphill bearing slightly left, away from the wood. At the brow of the hill, look for and head towards a single wooden post, where the path becomes better defined. Follow this path and look for two field gates in the valley below. Head to a point mid way between these, where a stile in the wall will become clear when you get closer. Cross the stile and go to the left.*

3. *Join a well-used track and go straight on down the valley with the dunes of the Warren on your right. At the car park by Candleston Castle, go out through the vehicular exit and follow the road back to Merthyr Mawr.*

4. *Pass the church on your left and take the road to the river on the right. Re-cross the footbridge and, immediately, take the path over the stile on the left. Go straight across the field and cross the River Ewenny on the high footbridge. At the main road, go right and take the first turning on the right to return to the car park.*

Variation
As for 1 then go left and continue at 4.

ACCESS BY BUS
National Welsh Bustler service V3 operates on the main road past the Castle.

19

LLANSANNOR CHURCH

Route 4   6 miles
(shorter variations of 5½ and 4 miles)
Cowbridge, Llansannor and Graig Penllyn

Outline   Cowbridge — Newton Moor — Llansannor — Graig Penllyn — Penllyn Castle — Cowbridge.

Summary   This walk explores a sleepy corner of the Vale of Glamorgan: flat meadowland surrounded by steep, often wooded, escarpments providing a number of short climbs en route. The variations suggested allow savings to be made in both distance and the amount of climbing, while still enjoying much of the variety of landscape and habitat.

Attractions   The Thaw valley north of Cowbridge broadens into a flat basin, similar in character to coastal 'levels', but here perched almost 100 feet above the sea. The basin is surrounded by limestone hills which, in parts, have been carved into steep escarpments rising to about 300 feet. Add a few small woods, coppices and avenues of trees and an attractive landscape results. Houses exist in moderation and generally of a style and character that enhance the scenery. In particular, the imposing Penllyn Castle, standing amongst trees on the brink of an escarpment, repeatedly attracts the eye.

Cowbridge was a Roman settlement, a medieval walled town, an ancient borough and the most important market town in the Vale of Glamorgan. It retains many interesting buildings: Porth Melin, the south gate of the town, dates from about 1300; Holy Cross church has an unusual octagonal tower; the Grammar School was founded in 1608, and there are many other buildings of 17th, 18th and 19th century origin. The streets, passages and courts of this pleasant town are worth exploring.

Heavy moorland meadows, well drained pasture on the surrounding hills, arable land, parkland, thicket and woodland provide a varied habitat, where the natural historian will find much to enjoy. The quiet and watchful stand a good chance of seeing a heron or, even, the flash of a kingfisher along the Thaw. In the wooded areas, it could be a jay or a green woodpecker. In places, limestone is exposed and fragments of crinoids (especially the stem segments, or ossicles, looking like small Polo mints) may be seen.

Refreshments   The Barley Mow, close to the half-way point, provides snacks or meals and has outside tables. There is a wide choice of eating places in Cowbridge.

Route 4
Cowbridge, Llansannor and Graig Penllyn   6 miles

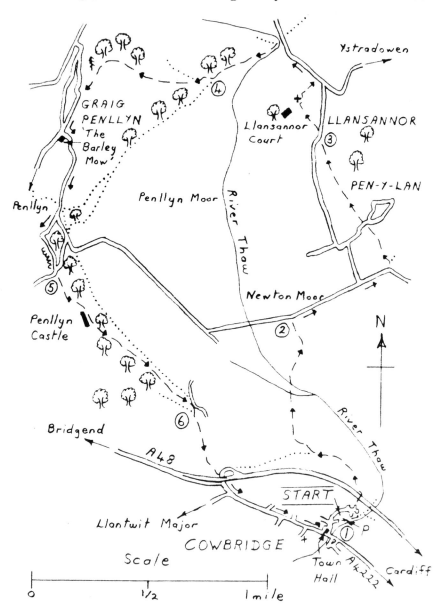

Route 4
Cowbridge, Llansannor and Graig Penllyn   6 miles
(shorter variations of 5½ and 4 miles)
START: *Car park behind the Town Hall in Cowbridge (O.S. Sheet 170 G.R. 996 747).*

ROUTE:
1. *From the south-east corner of the car park, take the path beside the river. At the second path left, go through a small housing estate to reach a track under the road viaduct. Go under the viaduct and up to and through a field gate followed by a pedestrian gate to the left of a farm. Cross a small field, go through another gate, bear left through the next gate then follow the left hand hedge. Where this turns left bear right to a kissing gate in the hedge on the right side of the field. Go through this gate and follow the fence in front to a gate at its left end. Go through this and straight down the field, cross a stile and head for a stile in the next boundary. Cross this stile–bridge–stile combination, another field and a similar combination. Go straight on until the adjacent stream bears right, then bear left through a gap in a hedge. Go straight on to and through a gate to a road.*
2. *Go right. 200 yards past a road to the left, go left 40 yards up a driveway to cross a stile on the left. Head for the top right corner of the field, cross a stile and go to the top left corner of the next field. Cross a stile and a narrow strip of rough ground to reach a road. Cross the stile opposite (if overgrown, there is a gateway 30 yards left), go straight on and over the next stile. Keep straight on, heading slightly downhill to a gate. Go through this, head for the left-most of two gates on the far side of the field and go out on to a road.*
3. *Go right, then left into 'Court Drive'. Where this turns left, go straight on to the churchyard. Pass to the right of the church, continue along an avenue to the right to a road and go left. Take the second track to the left, running at the foot of a scarp on its right, until a gate takes you into a garden.*
4. *The public footpath may not be clear, but, after 20 yards, go right, up a lawn, and enter the trees above. Bear half left, continue up to a small gate and out into a field. Head for a gate and stile near the diagonally opposite corner. Over the stile, follow a path through a wood, emerging at a gate into a field. Go down the field and through a gate on to a road. Follow the road ('The Rhiw') straight ahead and, at the junction by the pub, go left. At the next junction, go straight on and, at the T-junction, straight across, through a gate on a track.*

23

5. *Just before the next gate take a track to the left beside a high wall. Pass between some ruined buildings, through a gate and continue gradually down to a farm. Just before the gate on to the farm road, bear right up to and over a stile (if overgrown, the farm road acts as a 50-yard diversion).*
6. *Follow the left hand field boundary (crossing one stile) until this turns left. Go straight on to and through a kissing gate and down some steep steps. At the bottom, cross the road and go right, through the town to the Town Hall and the car park behind.*

Variation 1
As for 1 to 3 above but, at 4, go straight on, following the track at the foot of the scarp for a mile. When the track turns sharp left, bear right on a path along the bottom edge of a copse. At a road, go straight on, up steeply, to a junction, turn left and continue at 5.

Variation 2
As for 1 above but, at 2, turn left and follow the road to 5 and continue as before.

ACCESS BY BUS
Cardiff Bus (Service X2) operates frequently through Cowbridge.

GLAMORGAN CANAL

24

Route 5

3 miles
(shorter variation of 2 miles)

Forest Farm

Outline   Forest Farm — Glamorgan Canal — River Taff — Forest Farm.

Summary   This is something of an oasis in an urban environment. The walk follows two canals and the River Taff for much of its length, but still includes a mature woodland (mainly beech) and dense thicket areas, which are home to a variety of wildlife. The full walk has two gentle climbs, while the shorter variation is almost flat.

Attractions   A circular walk which goes around a modern industrial development and passes under a motorway twice may not sound interesting or inviting. However, the reality is surprisingly pleasant and rural.

Radyr weir on the River Taff was built to control the supply of water to the former Melingriffith Tin Plate Works, which was situated near the southern extremity of this walk. The weir has no industrial function now but forms a picturesque cascade on the river and you can picnic atop the fish pass—one of a number of recent steps taken to encourage migratory fish back to this river. Salmon are still rare . . . but you may be lucky enough to see one.

The first canal encountered on the walk is the 'feeder' which carried the water from above the weir: its size is indicative of the large volume of water required by the Tin Plate Works. The last remaining water-filled sections of the 200 year old Glamorganshire Canal seen on this walk are maintained as part of the nature reserve. Two locks have been partially restored and an original cast-iron tow path bridge remains. The two canals and adjacent wetland areas are home to a range of aquatic flora and fauna. In the summer, the Yellow Water-lily covers a large area of the canal.

An old tramroad forms the path beside the river and the bridge by which it crossed the Taff provides one of the best viewpoints for Castell Coch, the Red Castle. Close by the 18th century Forest Farmhouse is a short Nature Trail with a display board giving a good introduction to the environment of the nature reserve. There is a wide variety of trees on this walk—but can you find a walnut tree?

Refreshments   A couple of minutes off the route will get you to the Radyr Arms or the Asda superstore restaurant. There are picnic sites at the Forest Farm car park, by the weir and near the canal at the northern extremity of the route.

Route 5
Forest Farm

3 miles

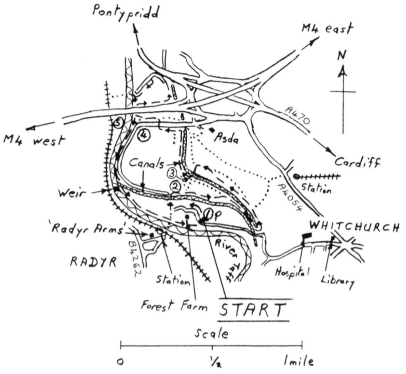

Pontypridd

M4 east

N↑

M4 west

A470

Asda

Cardiff

Canals

Station

A4054

Weir

WHITCHURCH

'Radyr Arms'

River Taff

RADYR

B4262

Station

Hospital   Library

Forest Farm   START

Scale

0   ½   1 mile

RIVER TAFF AND CASTLE COCH

26

Route 5
Forest Farm **3 miles**
(shorter variation of 2 miles)

START: *Car park at Forest Farm—take Velindre Road from 6-way roundabout on A4054 by Whitchurch Library (O.S. Sheet 171 G.R. 138 805).*

ROUTE

1. *Leave the car park and go right, passing the 'wildlife pond' on your right and the farm and butterfly garden on your left. At the end of the road, take the path to the right and, immediately after crossing the bridge over the feeder canal, take the track to the right. Where the track turns left, go straight ahead over the stile.*

2. *Follow the path with the canal on your right. Cross the next stile on to the Glamorgan Canal towpath and go to the right. Just after crossing the iron towpath bridge, join the track slightly above you on the left and follow this to the left as it climbs above the canal. At the end of the track, take the path which is straight ahead. After 100 yards, take the left hand fork: the path descends the steep slope and then climbs back up it. A path joins from the right and at the next junction go left, dropping down to the canal and crossing it on the footbridge. Turn right on the towpath.*

3. *Pass the lock on your right and continue along the towpath to the next lock, at the foot of the road embankment. Cross the stile on the left and go straight on until the path meets the road. Cross the road and take the bridlepath: follow this as it turns to the left where it is joined by a path from the right. Follow the bridlepath to where it crosses a track, then turn right along this, ignoring the path on your left.*

4. *Go under the motorway and take the path to the right. Follow this over two stiles until it rejoins the canal, then continue to the left beside the canal. Join the road and follow this past the subway on your right. After turning to the left go into the playing field on the left. Keep to the right side of the playing field and go through the kissing gate to rejoin the riverside path. Before heading to the left here, a few paces to the right and then left will take you on to the 'Ironbridge', a splendid viewpoint for Castell Coch. Return to where you left the playing field, go back under the motorway and take the path on the right by the river.*

5. *The route now follows the river past the weir and a footbridge to Radyr and eventually joins the road to Forest Farm. The car park entrance is a short distance to the left.*

27

Variation

As for 1 but do not cross the stile at the end. Instead go left and, where the track forks, go right, cross the stile ahead and continue to the towpath. Turn left and continue as 3 above. At 4, make a short diversion directly to the 'Ironbridge', return, then continue as 5 above.

ACCESS BY BUS OR TRAIN

Cardiff Bus has frequent services to Whitchurch (e.g. service 23) and Radyr (e.g. service 88). British Rail Valley Lines have regular services to Coryton (Whitchurch) and Radyr stations.

. . . A PICTURESQUE PANORAMA . . .

Route 6
4½ miles
(shorter variation of 3 miles)
Machen and Draethen

Outline   Machen — Coed Cefn-pwll-du — Draethen — Machen.

Summary   The first section of the walk has a long but generally gentle climb through a mixture of indigenous deciduous woodland and more recent conifer plantations. The route then explores the ridge, including a number of viewpoints, before dropping down into the Rhymney Valley at Draethen. The final leg back to Machen is fairly flat, through or beside farmland. The shorter variation curtails the ridge exploration.

Attractions
The forest of Coed Cefn-pwll-du covers an area that has seen coal mining to the north, while the limestone ridge in the south has been worked for lead since Roman times. The route passes close by the shafts of these early mines, which form a line along a contour just on the north side of the ridge. The fenced off shaft of one of the mines is adjacent to a seat at the viewpoint just before the route reaches the crest of the ridge.

The woodland could almost qualify as an arboretum. A large percentage is natural deciduous growth, including at least one giant beech (marked 'T' on the map, north of point 2 and 30 yards to the right of the path). If you are walking as a large family, you may like to find out how many people linking hands are needed to span its trunk. Some more recent planting is in small trial stands of both hard and soft wood and includes some unusual species.

The eastern side of the walk offers views of Mynydd Machen across the Rhymney Valley while, as the western-most extremity of the walk is neared, a picturesque panorama appears quite unexpectedly. The differing habitat around the route supports a wide variety of bird life. The sharp-eyed and quiet may well spot a jay in the forest or a heron along the river, but perhaps the most rewarding sight is a buzzard soaring: the steep wooded hillsides around Draethen are a popular hunting ground.

Refreshments   The Hollybush at Draethen is conveniently situated on the route, while the Maenllwyd Inn is only ¼ mile down the road from point 3. Both offer a range of snacks or meals.

Route 6
Machen and Draethen

4½ miles

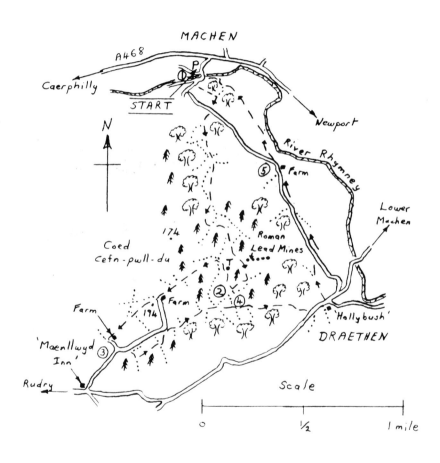

Route 6
Machen and Draethen

4½ miles
(shorter variation of 3 miles)

START: *Car park off The Crescent, Machen, behind the British Legion Club (O.S. Sheet 171 G.R. 210 891).*

ROUTE

1. *From the car park go left to the end of The Crescent, and then right over the River Rhymney. Follow the road which heads uphill and take the first path on the left (beside house No. 8). Keep straight on until you emerge on a drive then take the path to the right. At the road, go through the gate opposite on the forest track. While there are many tracks and paths to either side, the route keeps generally straight ahead on this prominent track for about a mile, rising steadily to the crest of the ridge. Just over the crest, go right on the first path which crosses the track. At the T-junction with a bridlepath go right.*

2. *The bridlepath emerges on to a track. Go right and take the first path on the left. Keep straight on to and through a gate into a field. Cross the field, passing just to the right of the farm buildings. At the corner of the field, go through the gate on the left, then immediately through a gate on the right. Keep the field boundary on your left and, at the end of the field, cross the stile. Go straight on and, over the brow of the hill, head just to the right of the farmhouse below. The field funnels down to a gate: go through this, turn left and follow the farm access road. At the T-junction, go left.*

3. *After 80 yards cross the stile on the right into the forest. Immediately, fork right, and at the crest of the ridge go left. At the next path junction, go right to a track and head left on this. The track turns right where there is an access from a road on the left. Keep to the track until it widens at a junction of tracks and take the bridlepath which bears slightly right: immediately pass a path on the right. At a T-junction, go right.*

4. *In a few yards, take the path to the left. The path falls steeply, passing one path to the right, to emerge from the forest by a cottage. Follow the drive to join the road and go left. At the road junction by the 'Hollybush', cross the stile on the left and follow the path. (From here to Machen the route has Rhymney Valley Ridgeway way-marking.) The second stile crossed lets you on to the road: head left for ½ mile to Rhyd-y-Gwern Farm.*

5. *Just past the farm, cross the stile on the right. The path crosses another stile and heads straight on down the hill. Walk with a copse on your right, then cross a footbridge and stile and follow the field boundary to the left. Go through the kissing gate into the playing field and follow the left boundary. Leaving the playing field, the route crosses a footbridge, passes through a*

31

*kissing gate and skirts a market garden before emerging on to a track via
another kissing gate. Go right and, at a T-junction, left. At the road, turn
right over the river, then left to return to the car park.*

Variation
As for 1 but go left on the bridlepath at the end. At the track go right and
immediately take the bridlepath to the left. At the next junction, bear left and
continue as 4 above.

ACCESS BY BUS
National Welsh service 50 or Bustler C9 operate on the main road through
Machen at least hourly.

BOX GATE

Route 7

5½ miles

(shorter variations of 3 and 4½ miles)

Rudry

Outline   Rudry Common — Rhymney Valley Ridgeway Footpath — Rudry — Rudry Common.

Summary   The walk provides a wide variety of woodland and heath scenery: the different natural habitats support a correspondingly wide range of birds and animals. There is a moderate climb up to the Ridgeway long-distance footpath and two or three further short climbs. From the ridge there are views of Cardiff and the Bristol Channel, Caerphilly and the Rhymney Valley and, on clear days, the main peaks of the Brecon Beacons. Two shorter variations are suggested.

Attractions   The most striking feature of the Common is its pock-marked appearance, like a giant's pin-cushion. The many small craters are the remains of 'bell pits'—mini coal mines worked by one or two people using simple tools and a hand-operated windlass. Between the summit of Mynydd Rudry and the southern edge of the Common, all the seams of the South Wales coalfield break the surface. Initially, coal was worked from the outcrop and such activity is apparent from bands across the upper slopes of Mynydd Rudry. Once the 'easy' coal had been won, the next step was to dig down to the seams where they were still quite shallow: hence the 'bell pits'.

Perhaps one measure of the variety of the flora is the number of edible fruits which exist in the area. At the appropriate time of year, you may see on this walk wild strawberries, raspberries, blackberries, wild damson, sweet chestnut and hazel nuts. Home-winemakers may wish to add the elder and blackthorn (sloe gin?) to the list.

The cover on the Common ranges from coarse grass to bracken to gorse and broom to small trees, notably the sessile oak which has found one area disturbed by coal working particularly to its liking: the last leg of the walk skirts this small wood.

In the summer, the area of the Common between the car park and Mynydd Rudry is a bracken-covered maze of paths. This, coupled with the bell pit craters and the natural contours, provides a superb venue for hide-and-seek—be sure to allow time for a game.

Refreshments   The Griffin and the Maenllwyd offer bar snacks and full restaurant facilities and both have outside tables. There is a picnic site beside the car park on the Common.

33

Route 7
Rudry

5½ miles

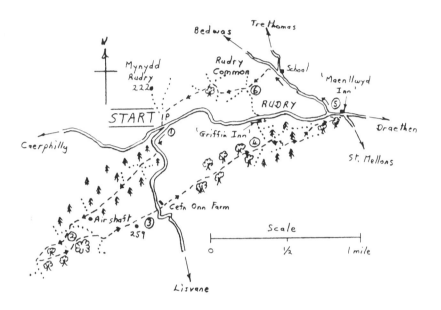

A BELL PIT

34

Route 7
Rudry
5½ miles
(shorter variations of 3 and 4½ miles)

START: *Car park on Rudry Common beside the minor road from Caerphilly (take Van Road from junction by main post office) to Rudry (O.S. Sheet 171 G.R. 183 865).*

ROUTE

1. *Take the small side road opposite the car park. Shortly after leaving the Common, enter the forest on the right via the 'box' gate (designed for horses, as this is a bridleway). After 300 yards where the track forks, bear left to stay just inside the woodland. Keep to the main track and in about ½ mile look out for the airshaft, ventilating the Rhymney Valley railway tunnel, about 50 yards off to the left. Continue straight on and leave the forest at the next 'box' gate. Turn right.*

2. *Immediately on your left are the remains of some limekilns. Take the winding track which bears off to the left and heads gradually up on to the ridge. At the top, you will see a field gate with a pedestrian gate to its right: do not go through the gates, but turn sharp left along the ridge. (This is part of the Rhymney Valley Ridgeway Footpath and the blue or yellow arrows help to define our route to point 4.) Keep to the way which follows the ridge, ignoring any side tracks. Pass the disused quarry on your right, and the second gate you pass through brings you to the road by Cefn Onn Farm.*

3. *Cross the road and go through two stiles to skirt around the right of the farm. Go straight up the bank beyond the second stile and head straight on, keeping the fence immediately on your left. The scrubby bushes on your right gradually change to more substantial trees and you enter woodland: keep generally straight ahead. When you come to a field, the track bears left to keep just inside the wood. After a steep downhill section, cross the stile and go through the field gate some 50 yards ahead.*

4. *Go straight on for a few paces, then take the path on your right which has a fence on its right. The path takes a turn to the left and soon leads into a steep zig-zag descent with steps and handrails. At the track at the bottom, turn left. Go straight on at the next junction, then take the path which bears left up on to the ridge. At the top, turn right and follow the track until it emerges on to the road 150 yards west of the Maenllwyd Inn.*

5. *Follow the road opposite, signed to Rudry Village. In about ½ mile pass the school and a road on your right. Just beyond, take the track on the*

35

left which leads on to and along the southern edge of the Common, until you draw level with a kissing gate on your left.

6. *Choose the path which bears slightly to the right away from the hedge. At the junction with another path beside the small wood, turn right. At the junction of tracks by the northern corner of the wood, turn left over the stile into the field. The path now skirts the edge of the wood to your left. Cross the stile back on to the Common and continue straight ahead back to the car park.*

Variation 1

As for 1 and 2 above but, at 3, turn left and follow the road back to the car park.

Variation 2

As for 1 to 3 above but, at 4, turn left down the hill. At the bottom, cross the stile and follow the narrow path to emerge by The Griffin Motel. At the road, turn right and, at the front of the pub, take the steep path down on the left. Go through the kissing gate and follow the path diagonally up the field. Emerge on to the Common through another kissing gate, turn left and continue from 6 above.

ACCESS BY BUS

National Welsh Bustler (Service C3) from Caerphilly goes past the Common.

GARTH HILL

36

Route 8

(shorter variation of 3½ miles)

Gwaelod-y-Garth

Outline   Mountain Road — Garth Hill — Gwaelod-y-Garth — Mountain Road.

Summary   The walk involves two stiff climbs of about 400 feet, one at the start and the other at the end. The initial effort is rewarded with splendid views. The lower parts of the route are in varied woodland, and include a riverside section and clues to former industrial activity. The shorter variation halves the final uphill section.

Attractions   Garth Hill just achieves 'mountain' status by courtesy of the tumulus at its high point. It provides a birds-eye view of the Taff valley, with the villages appearing like models complete with toy cars and trains. Longer distance views are afforded, to the south, across the Bristol Channel to the English Coast from the Mendips round to Exmoor and, to the north, to Pen-y-Fan, the highest point in the Brecon Beacons. On an autumn day, with long shadows, the panorama can be magnificent. Try to pick out the fairy-tale Castle Coch, on the south-east shoulder of the Taff Gorge, and Caerphilly Castle off to the east.

In the nineteenth century, Gwaelod-y-Garth was a busy industrial community. There were a number of coal mines, while iron, and limestone, for flux, were mined or quarried from the Lesser Garth to the south. These were linked by tramroads to the iron works, which had 3 blast furnaces, 82 coke ovens and 11 puddling furnaces when it closed. Mercifully, in the last 100 years, nature, with a little help from man, has worked a small miracle. An enquiring eye will find evidence of the industrial past, but the area now provides a wide variety of indigenous trees and flowers (at their best in the spring) and a haven for birds and animals. If you have time, visit the little-known nature reserve which can be entered from the road called 'Georgetown', just south of point 4 on the route.

Try making the walk an I-spy game. Can you spot the two castles, Taff's Well spring, a colliery entrance tunnel, a piece of coal, 10 different flowers, 20 varieties of tree (harder in the winter) and crystals of calcite?

Refreshments   The Gwaelod-y-Garth Inn offers limited light snacks: more substantial refreshments can be had at The Taff's Well: both have outside tables. There is a picnic area near the Mountain Road car park.

37

Route 8
Gwaelod-y-Garth   4½ miles

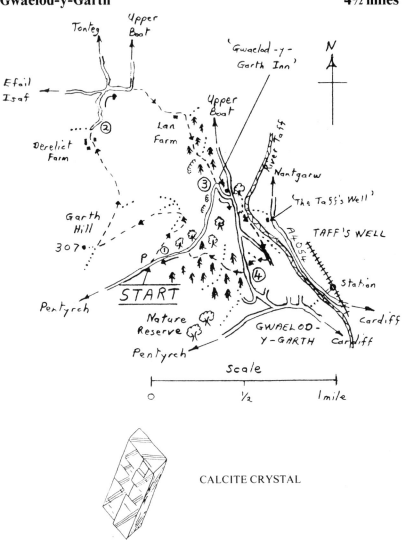

CALCITE CRYSTAL

Garth. There are more frequent services operating through Taff's Well (e.g. Cardiff Bus route 26) and British Rail Valley Lines run frequent services on weekdays and Saturdays: footbridges across the River Taff near the station and The Taff's Well inn give access to the walk.

Route 8

Gwaelod-y-Garth

4½ miles

(shorter variation of 3½ miles)

START: *Grass block layby on Mountain Road between Gwaelod-y-Garth and Pentyrch—leave A470 at first junction north of M4 (O.S. Sheet 171 G.R. 108 833).*

ROUTE

1. *Just down the road from the layby, take the path which heads gradually up to and then around the east end of Garth Hill. From the highest point above the precipitous drop down to the River Taff, take the path which bears left towards the broad crest of the hill and then head for the far tumulus, crowned by a triangulation point. Just short of this, turn right on to the well-defined track down the north flank to the start of the surfaced road just below the derelict farm buildings.*

2. *Continue downhill on the road: at the first junction turn right and at the second go straight on. When the road turns sharp left, go straight on through the gate and follow the farm access track. Pass through Lan Farm between the buildings with right, left, right and left turns in quick succession. Go through the gate and follow the track along the top edge of the forest, and then straight down through the woods to the road at a hair-pin bend.*

3. *Turn left and, at the T-junction by the inn, turn right. After 100 yards, take the steep zig-zag path down to the river bank. Do not use the subway (unless to view the murals or to cross the river) but go to the right beside the river. At the path junction fork right (a 30 yard detour to the left here provides a view across the river of the tepid spring, marked by brown-stained blockstone, from which Taff's Well takes its name). At the road, turn left. Shortly, take the path on the right, then follow the path to the left, passing an old drift mine entrance. At the road, go straight across.*

4. *The path bears left then bends round to the right. Go through the kissing gate and head up through the woods. At the slightly offset path crossing go straight on, continuing upwards to the top edge of the forest. Go through the gate, straight across the field and through the kissing gate on to the road. Turn left to complete the walk.*

Variation

As for 1 and 2 above but, at 3, turn right and follow the road back to the start.

ACCESS BY BUS OR TRAIN

Cardiff Bus Clipper (service 139) is a sparse weekday service to Gwaelod-y-

continued opposite

LLANTRISANT COMMON

Route 9

3 miles

(shorter variations of 1½ or 2 miles)

Llantrisant

Outline Llantrisant — The Common — Y Graig — Llantrisant — The Common — Llantrisant.

Summary This walk around Llantrisant provides pleasant views to all points of the compass. The route passes through the varied countryside of the Common, Y Graig and farmland. There are a number of short climbs on the route and one longer, moderately graded, up Y Graig. The walk can be conveniently split into two halves, offering the possibility of a shorter walk coupled with an exploration of the cobbled lanes and alleyways of the old town.

Attractions Llantrisant sits astride the ridge which marks the southern rim of the coalfield. Despite the industrialisation of the area, the heart of the town retains its character, with narrow lanes and alleys, interesting old buildings and the church on the crest of the ridge forming a natural focal point and a landmark in the area.

Llantrisant is the home of the Royal Mint, though this is located on the industrial estate north of the Common and is better viewed from a distance. However, the Mint has a permanent exhibition at Model House in the Bull Ring in the old town. The exhibition shows a history of coin making since the 17th century, with machinery and displays of coins and medals. Sorry—no free samples of current coinage, but proof coins and souvenirs are on sale

Model House itself is an interesting conversion of a 19th century workhouse into a craft and design centre, where you can see craftsmen in action with skills as diverse as ceramics, furniture making and film animation. The building also includes the Coffee Shop, which provides refreshments and panoramic views across the Vale of Glamorgan.

The route passes through a variety of habitats: the poorly-drained acid soils of the Common contrast with the steep bracken-covered slopes of Y Graig and the more gentle slopes to the east of the town. You can expect to see a wide range of flowers at any time, but look out for a field with a grand display of foxgloves in the spring. Ponies roam the Common and you may see rabbits if you are quiet enough. However, if you miss the real thing, there is a quite confusing proliferation of yellow bunny signs in the area—how many of these do you pass on route?

Refreshments The Coffee Shop at Model House or try one of the pubs around the Bull Ring.

41

Route 9
Llantrisant

3 miles

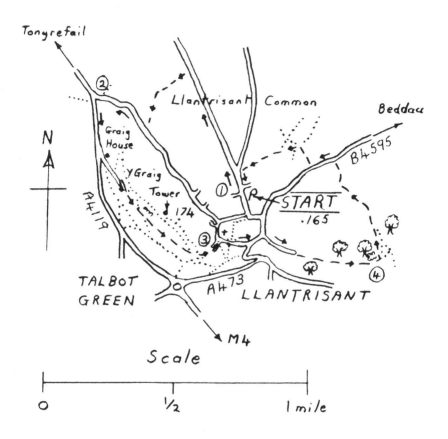

Tonyrefail

② .

Llantrisant Common

Beddau

N

B4595

Graig House

y Graig Tower

A4119

174

①

P

START

.165

③

④

TALBOT GREEN

A473

LLANTRISANT

M4

Scale

0   ½   1 mile

go up Common Road and through the town to just south of the church then continue from 3 (1½ miles). Detailed directions through the town are not given: it is a place to explore freely and too small to get lost in.
ACCESS BY BUS
Llantrisant is well served by National Welsh buses—services 241, 244 and Bustler G4.

Route 9

Llantrisant

3 miles

(shorter variations of 1½ or 2 miles)

START: *Car park off Common Road (Heol-y-Sarn), 200 yards north of the Bull Ring where Model House is situated (O.S. Sheet 170 G.R. 048 836).*

ROUTE:

1. *From the car park go down Common Road to gain access on to the Common by the cattle grid. Walking on the Common beside the road, continue straight on for ½ mile then take the first prominent track to the left. Head straight into an apex formed by two hedge lines: go through a kissing gate and up a track to a road. Turn right and follow the road downhill to the junction with the main road. Cross carefully to the footpath and turn left.*

2. *Follow the main road for 200 yards then, again with care, cross to go up the drive to the right of Graig House. Keep to the drive for 150 yards then take a path which diverges to the left and passes just above a cottage. Continue on this path until Llantrisant is reached. (The energetic may prefer the more strenuous climb to the tower at the summit of Y Graig: while there is a choice of paths to the tower, they all bring you back to 3.)*

3. *Go through the gate and along the narrow cul de sac (Heol-y-Graig) with a row of cottages on the left. Pass a road on your right, then go right at two T-junctions in quick succession. Keep straight on until the main road into Llantrisant is reached. Follow this to the left for 100 yards, then take a small road on the right (ignoring the 'private road' signs). Just after passing Erw Hir House on the left take a path which bears slightly right and downhill. Go through a kissing gate and follow the path along the top of a field. Beyond the next kissing gate, the path bears slightly left and drops downhill.*

4. *Just before the slope temporarily levels out, take a path to the left through old tips and a quarry cutting. Bear left to keep rising and ignore any side paths until the path goes through a kissing gate to join a track. Follow this as it passes behind some houses to join the Beddau road. Go left on the verge for 100 yards. Just before the first house on the right, cross the main road and take a track to the right. Go through the kissing gate by a cottage on to the Common and take the track to the left to the cattle grid on Common Road. Go left to return to the car park.*

Variations

As for 1 and 2 then return to the car park through the old town (2 miles) OR

continued opposite

CWM DU OAK WOODS

(a) Stigmarian root   (b) Lepidodendron,   (c) Calamites stem.
                                 bark of trunk   (Giant horsetail)

TREE FOSSILS

44

Route 10

5½ miles
(shorter variation of 3½ miles)

Pont Rhyd-y-Cyff

Outline   Pont Rhyd-y-Cyff — Moel Cynhordy — Garw Forest — Cwm Du — Pont Rhyd-y-Cyff.

Summary   The walk starts with a mile of steady climbing but, thereafter, the going is fairly easy. The second quarter of the walk, being between 1000 and 1200 feet above sea level, reaps the benefit of the early exertion, with views of some of the best scenery in The Valleys. The return half of the route follows the peaceful valley of the Nant Cwm-du. The shorter variation enjoys many of the features of the full route.

Attractions   The Llynfi valley is not typical of the South Wales Valleys: it is wider, more open and gently contoured, reflecting its Welsh name, which means smooth. It has been able to accommodate development more comfortably amongst quiet sheep farms, while the efforts of nature and man have healed many of the industrial scars. The result is some beautiful and varied scenery, ideal for walking.

The western escarpment of Moel Cynhordy is decorated by a line of small spoil heaps, marking the long-abandoned working of a coal outcrop. The route climbs up to the northern end of this line where one old adit, at least, now acts as a spring. Further on, the walk skirts the much larger spoil heap of a recently closed mine. It will be some years before vegetation helps this to blend in with the scenery, but it does offer the opportunity of finding a fossil or two. Plant fossils are common in the coal measures, especially in the darker shales. Look for the impressions of leaves, twigs, bark and roots—calamites, lepidodendron and stigmarian roots are perhaps most easily recognised. The area of the walk is very quiet: do not be surprised if you do not meet anyone. But these are ideal conditions for bird-watching and enjoying the varied plant life. This is good country for buzzards and there is a fine example of a natural sessile oak woodland in the lower part of Cwm Du.

Refreshments   Bar snacks can be had at The Tylers Arms, which has a pleasant stream-side beer garden, or the old village of Llangynwyd ('Llan' on signs), a mile away across the Llynfi Valley and worth a visit itself, has two comfortable inns. But, on a nice day, an alfresco meal en route might be preferred.

45

Route 10
Pont Rhyd-y-Cyff

5½ miles

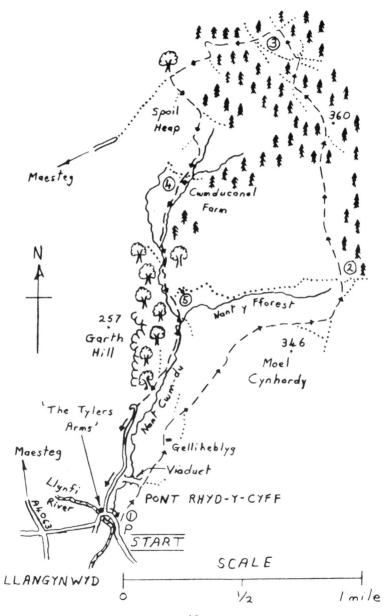

Maesteg

Spoil
Heap

360

④

Cwmduconal
Farm

N

⑤

Nant y Fforest

257
·
Garth
Hill

346
·
Moel
Cynhordy

'The Tylers
Arms'

Nant Cwm-du

Maesteg

Gelliheblyg

Llynfi
River

Viaduct

A4063

PONT RHYD-Y-CYFF

①
P
START

LLANGYNWYD

SCALE

0   ½   1 mile

Route 10
Pont Rhyd-y-Cyff
5½ miles
(shorter variation of 3½ miles)

START: *Hard area beside road, just east of village, at entrance to track to Gelliheblyg—leave A4063 just north of Llangynwyd Post Office (O.S. Sheet 170 G.R. 874 890).*

ROUTE:

1. *Follow the track northwards, passing through a gate and over the disused railway to the right of the viaduct. 150 yards past Gelliheblyg, go through a gate on the right to take the track rising gradually towards the north end of Moel Cynhordy. After the next gate, the track passes through some old spoil heaps and bears left before making a long curve to the right. Pass through another gate and by two more spoil heaps. Then, after 150 yards, take an indistinct path diverging left towards a stile. Cross the stile—the path rises for 100 yards then heads left and down towards the nearest corner of the forest. Just before the forest, cross a stile on the left and follow the forest boundary northwards.*

2. *When the forest veers to the right, bear left towards a gate in the fenceline ahead. Go through the gate and straight on to the top left corner of the field. Cross a stile into the forest and follow the track straight on. Head left at the first junction and right at the second. In quick succession, go left at a Y-junction, left at a track crossing and straight on at a crossing, on to a little used track with a wall on its right. At the next junction go left.*

3. *Cross the next track and go left on a lower track: immediately take a track to the right, dropping steeply down. 100 yards after a sharp bend to the left, go through a gate on the right. Go through a second gate and down a field, parallel to the fence on the left. The path becomes a track in a shallow cutting. As a fence looms ahead, climb out on the left to cross a stile, then go left on a track. Pass the big spoil heap, then take the track which bears right around the foot of the heap. After 200 yards go to the left, with a drainage ditch on your left. Just after the ditch—now stone-lined—turns right, pick up a track running down to a gate. Go through to Cwmducanol Farm.*

4. *Go straight on, passing immediately to the right of the farmhouse and leaving via a gate. Follow the track through two more gates, cross a stream (collapsed bridge provides stepping stones) and then, at a T-junction, go left. At the next junction go right.*

5. *Cross a stile by the next gate and follow the fence on the right. Go through a gate on the right, cross a bridge and head left. Fork right to rise slightly into the woods then keep straight ahead, ignoring minor paths to the side. After going through a gate, the path passes to the left of a ruined building and a path joins from the right. Keep straight on to emerge via a gate on to a road at a hairpin bend. Follow the road to the left down into Pont Rhyd-y-Cyff and, by The Tylers Arms, go left to return to the start.*

Variation

As for 1, then, after 100 yards, turn away from the forest and cross the field (aim just to the right of Garth Hill) to join a track in a strip of rough ground. Go left and follow this track down to a farm. Pass just above and then down beside the farmhouse. At the junction, go straight on and continue at 5.

ACCESS BY BUS

There are frequent National Welsh services (Nos 232 and 236) on the A4063 through Llangynwyd.

RHONDDA FAWR

48

Route 11

4 miles
(shorter variation of 2½ miles)

Llwynypia Mountain

Outline   Nant-y-Gwiddon — Llwynypia Mountain — Clydach Vale — Gelli — Nant-y-Gwiddon.

Summary   The walk starts with a steep climb beside Nant-y-Gwiddon. This is the hardest part of the route, although there are three more uphill sections in the next two miles, each leading to completely fresh views. Emerging from the dense forest on to a sheer-sided crag above Llwynypia is an experience not to be missed—and even the shorter variation ensures that it is not.

Attractions   The Rhondda is the most densely developed of the coal mining valleys, with each community merging with its neighbours along the valley floor to produce what has been described as 'the longest street'. Yet, in the early 19th century, the area was sparsely populated and would have compared favourably with other mountain areas of scenic beauty. One can get a feel for what it was like by climbing on to the adjacent mountains, where the impact of development and mining activity is greatly diminished. This walk around the summit of Llwynypia Mountain achieves this objective. The lower slopes seen in the early part of the walk support deciduous woodland of the sort that would have been far more extensive 150 years ago. The coniferous plantations higher up have no link with the last century, but are a softening feature in a sometimes rugged landscape. They are also extremely dense in places, so that the path remains dark and cool on the hottest summer day: a blessing on two of the uphill sections.

After the first of these dark climbs, the route emerges suddenly on to a small precipitous crag high above Llwynypia (young children may wish to reassure nervous parents by holding their hands at this point!). The views here are southwards down the Rhondda Fawr and eastwards across the Rhondda Fach to the St. Gwynno Forest. The next views are of Cwm Clydach and then, as the route heads north, the Rhondda Fawr appears rising north-west to its source above Craig y Llyn, at a height approaching 2000 feet.

Between the last two viewpoints, the route drops down briefly to a small park at Clydach Vale, where the children's play area may be appreciated by youngsters.

Refreshments   Nothing on route, but Tonypandy, 2 miles to the south, offers a choice of eating options.

Route 11
Llwynypia Mountain

4 miles

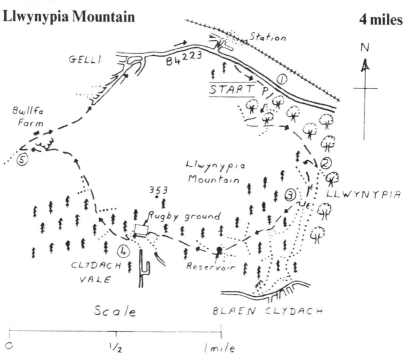

LLWYNYPIA MOUNTAIN

Route 11
Llwynypia Mountain
4 miles
(shorter variation of 2½ miles)

START: *Craig Nant-y-Gwiddon car park on B4223 ¾ mile north of Llywnypia (O.S. Sheet 170 G.R. 988 945).*

ROUTE

1. *Climb up the valley side beside the stream. At a slight shelf where the main path goes left to cross the stream, continue upwards to a path junction above the tree line. Go left, cross the stream and continue on the path, just above the oak woodland. As the conifer forest nears, carefully pass a 4 feet wide cleft just to the left of the path. The path continues at the lower edge of the conifers then, as it curves to the right, take a path which turns back sharply to the right.*

2. *The path rises in the forest, with one sharp turn back to the left. As the gradient eases, ignore any paths to the right and emerge at a viewpoint crag. Continue for about 200 yards to another viewpoint crag, then go right to join a forest track.*

3. *Go right for 20 yards, then sharp left on a path. Go straight on at a stream crossing, ignoring paths to the left beside it. The path rises to emerge at a clearing at a junction of tracks. Go straight ahead, pass to the left of a reservoir (looking like the remnant of some old castle), then take a path which diverges to the left. Where the path forks, go left, down to and through a gate into the park. Go right, pass above the bowling green, then left, beside it. Head right just below the rugby pitch and leave the park via a gate. Go straight on to a footbridge then up to join a forest track.*

4. *Go right. Pass a path to the left and a track to the right. Keep straight on with a high fence on your right. When the main track turns left, go straight on, cross a stile on to open land and continue straight ahead. After 200 yards, the path swings to the left just above the remains of an earth ditch and wall. Take care to pass above the unfenced quarry before the path drops down to a track.*

5. *Go sharp right and follow the track past Bwllfa Farm and through two gates. Continue straight on—the track is now a road—follow this until it bears right to a T-junction. Go left and, at the main road, cross to the footpath and head right. Just after a modern housing estate on the left, cross the road to a path which leads back to the car park.*

51

Variation

As for 1 and 2 above but, at 3, go left and follow the track down to Blaen Clydach. At the junction with a road, go sharp left and, immediately, take a lane diverging to the left behind some houses. At the end of the lane, continue on a path at the edge of the forest. Go sharp right across a stream, fork left then go sharp left on a path climbing up a small spur. 40 yards after the power line clearing, take a path to the right and follow this for ½ mile to rejoin the outward route at 2. Re-trace the first section of the route.

ACCESS BY BUS OR TRAIN

Frequent train services to Ystrad Rhondda station. There are no buses on the B4223, but National Welsh serves Gelli, Ystrad, Llwynypia and Clydach Vale.

ST. GWYNNO'S CHURCH

52

Route 12

4 miles
(shorter variation of 2 miles)

Llanwonno

Outline   Llanwonno — St. Gwynno Forest — Cefn Gwyngul — Llanwonno.

Summary   The route wanders in and out of the St. Gwynno Forest visiting a number of viewpoints. The car park is 1000 feet above sea level and there are a number of short climbs on the walk, taking it to 1350 feet at its highest. While coniferous trees dominate the topography, rows of beeches and the ongoing felling and replanting make the forest far from dull and a variety of plants and birds may be seen. A shorter option is offered.

Attractions   Llanwonno has just two buildings: the Church of St. Gwynno and the Brynfynnon Hotel—keys to the former can be obtained at the latter. There has been a place of worship here for 14 centuries and one Griffith Morgan is buried in the graveyard. Reputed to be the fastest runner in the world, when he beat 'Prince' from Bedwas over 12 miles in a time of 53 minutes, he collapsed and died, so the tale is told, when his sweetheart patted him on the back in congratulation. The legend is commemorated by the Nos Galan races on New Year's Eve.

Early in the walk, views across and down Cwm Clydach are afforded. Crossing to the west side of Cefn Gwyngul, leaves the Rhondda Valleys open to inspection—and there can be few better vantage points. The final part of the route shows off the forest itself, looking over the valley of the Clydach and a number of its tributaries, with a reservoir in the centre. The vistas change with the season and as a result of forest management, so this is an area to return to time and again.

Despite its height, much of the area is well sheltered and you may see a field of barley at 1000 feet. It is also a good area for wild raspberries and blackberries. While mature coniferous forests can be short of wildlife, here the patchwork of trees of various types and age and cleared areas is much better populated. Look out for tree fossils in the pennant sandstone: while the specimens found in sandstone are generally weathered and less easy to identify, they are relatively common.

The route passes one of the most dominant landmarks in the area, a truncated pyramidal peak. Its regular shape gives it away as man made—a remodelled colliery spoil tip—even though it has a green face. Can you find a 'dry-stone' cross on route?

Refreshments   The Brynfynnon Hotel offers a range of refreshments.

53

Route 12
Llanwonno

4 miles

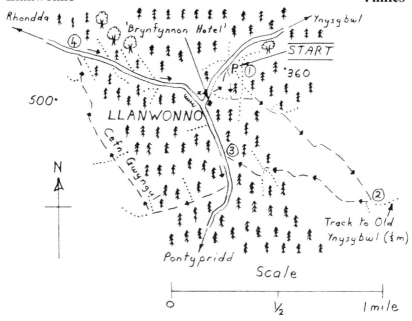

FOSSILS IN PENNANT SANDSTONE

Route 12

Llanwonno

4 miles
(shorter variation of 2 miles)

START: *Forestry car park, 300 yards north-east of the Brynfynnon Hotel—take the B4273 from Pontypridd and turn left just north of Old Ynysybwl (O.S. Sheet 170 G.R. 032 958).*

ROUTE

1. *Facing the road, 20 yards from the entrance to the car park, take a path to the left then go left again immediately, skirting the forest. After 200 yards, go over a stile on the left and follow the path across one track and up to a second, then go right. As the track completes a bend to the left, cross a stile on the right. Bear slightly left across a field to meet the top fenceline at the second gate along it. Go through this and head right, making a long diagonal crossing of the field to meet the track along the top by the gate at the far end. Go through the gate, right through another gate, then straight on.*

2. *The track winds across a valley and re-enters the forest at a gate. Continue up-hill, crossing another track at a sharp bend to the left. At the next junction, go right and continue to the road.*

3. *Head left and take the first track to the right. Pass a track to the right and continue to a cattle grid at the edge of the forest. Cross the adjacent stile, go straight on for 30 yards then head right. The path is poorly defined, so aim for the right side of the pyramidal tip and pick up a clearer track on the approach to a gate. Cross the stile by the gate and continue as the track bends to right and left. At a junction, go straight on through a gate and, via another gate, to the road. Turn right.*

4. *Follow the road down to Llanwonno (there is a path on the left verge for most of the way). At the junction by the pub, go left, then take the path straight ahead over the small hill, back to the start.*

Variation

As for 1 and 2 but, at 3, go right and follow the road to Llanwonno. By the pub, go right and take the path over the hill, as described at 4.

ACCESS BY BUS

There is no public transport to Llanwonno but the route can be joined at point 2 from Old Ynysybwl (National Welsh Bustler Service Y3), which is ½ mile away.

TAFF VALE RAILWAY

Route 13   4 miles
Quaker's Yard

Outline   Quaker's Yard — Pont-y-Gwaith — Glamorgan Canal — Quaker's Yard.

Summary   The majority of the walk traces a canal and a tramroad, so gradients are gentle except for two short climbs. Industrial archaeology is the dominant theme, but this is a picturesque section of the Taff Valley and all interests in natural history can be satisfied.

Attractions   Quaker's Yard takes its name from the 17th century Friend's burial ground by the main cross-roads in the village. In Quaker tradition, no graves are marked; but one stray gravestone exists, dated more than 100 years later than the last known burial.

Anyone with a feel for our industrial heritage will experience a tingle in the soles of his feet throughout this walk. The route starts and finishes on the track of the Penydarren tramroad, where the first steam locomotive to run on rails hauled 10 tons of iron and passengers from Merthyr to Abercynon in 1804. The tramroad closed over 100 years ago, but well-preserved sections of rail support stones remain: can you find where the track diverged at passing places? The walk uses one of two tramroad bridges over the Taff dating from 1815, having replaced the original timber structures when one collapsed.

Early on, the route passes under the graceful curving twin viaducts of the Taff Vale railway and, later, the rock cutting just south of the viaducts can be seen. The cutting was formed when the original rope-worked incline from Abercynon was replaced in 1864 by a 1 in 40 gradient suitable for normal traction locomotives. Edwardsville was once a major junction on the Great Western and Rhymney cross valley railway. Of this, the remains of two viaducts, a cutting and the tunnel through to the Cynon Valley can be seen on the walk. The stone bridge at Pont-y-Gwaith is the work of the 18th century architect, William Edwards, famous for the splendid crossing from which Pontypridd takes its name. At the time of writing, Pont-y-Gwaith was near collapse, closed even to pedestrians—a serious problem on this circular route! The County Council advise that it should re-open in the Spring of 1992. On the west side of the Taff, the route follows the line of the Glamorgan Canal, opened in 1794 to serve the Cyfartha Ironworks in Merthyr and closed about 100 years later. The crumbling last canal bridge, the location of former locks and the 'Prince Llewellyn' (the tavern at the top of the 204 foot climb from Abercynon, now a private house) can all be seen. Do not be deterred if this talk of past engineering achievements leaves you

continued on page 60

57

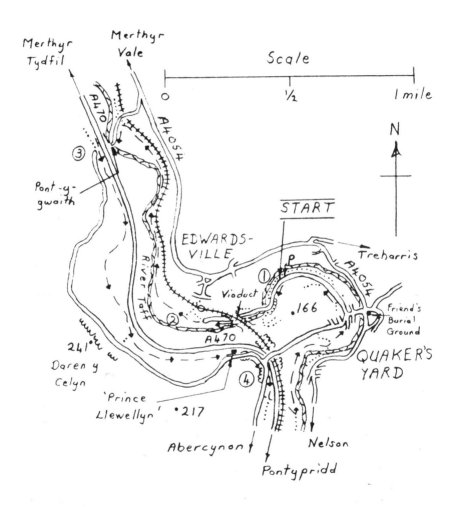

Route 13
Quaker's Yard   4 miles
START: *Layby on single track lane—take second right after crossing River Taff bridge from A4054 and keep right (O.S. Sheets 170 & 171 G.R. 092 967).*

ROUTE:

1. *Continue up the valley on the lane (the tramroad), cross the river and pass under the railway viaduct. Just after the tarmac surface ends, pass two houses, and keep straight ahead through two gates.*

2. *Follow the track past the remains of two demolished viaducts then, over the next ½ mile, evidence of its original function becomes frequent. When the track diverges, go left. Cross a stile on to a road and head left down to the river. Go over the bridge, up a track to the right and through the subway under the A470 (is there an echo?). The track rises to a gate on to the end of a road with tracks going to each side on the line of the old canal. Go left.*

3. *Pass through two gates, to the left of an old canal bridge and over the tunnel through to the Cynon Valley (marked by the deep cutting on the left). The route diverts to the right to skirt above a cutting on the A470, returning to the course of the canal at the second stile. Pass by the Prince Llewellyn, join the road and go left, over a cattle grid, to a junction. Go left to the railway bridge to see the rock cutting, then return to the junction and head left.*

4. *Take the path on the left, behind the crash barrier, leading down some steps to a track (back on the canal line at the site of a flight of locks). Pass a track to the right then take a track to the left, under the A470 and railway. Go through a gate and bear half right to follow a path down towards the river. At a path junction, go sharp left. As the path drops, fork left then continue to re-join the tramroad just left of a bridge over the river. Go left, straight across the road by 'Tollgate House' and follow the lane back to the start.*

ACCESS BY BUS OR TRAIN
Quaker's Yard is well served by National Welsh buses (e.g. service X78). There is a good train service to Quaker's Yard station (at Edwardsville, surprisingly) from where a short footpath links to the route at 2. Even if travelling by car, children might prefer to start and end with a 1½ mile train ride between Abercynon and Quaker's Yard.

cold. The scenery is pleasant—steep wooded valley sides, overlooked by Daren-y-Celyn with its Giant's Bite, and attractive views. Come for the spring flowers or the autumn colours. Birds are plentiful, rabbits and squirrels abound to reward the quiet and watchful and fragments of tree fossils can be seen in the pennant sandstone.

Refreshments There are picnic tables by the river near the start and two pubs in Quaker's Yard, but those with children might find the Railway Inn, two miles away, on the road to Nelson more suitable.

PARC CWM DARRAN LAKE

60

Route 14

4½ miles
(shorter variations of 2 and 1½ miles)

Parc Cwm Darran

Outline   Deri — Cefn-y-Brithdir — Parc Cwm Darran — Deri.

Summary   To gain the ridge of Cefn-y-Brithdir, the walk starts with a climb: fairly steep in places in the first ½ mile and relatively gentle for the next mile. But then it is all down hill! Do not rush the climb—enjoy the views that unfold on the way, though the most spectacular panorama only appears as the ridge is reached. The route passes through deciduous woodland and conifer forest, with open moorland on the ridge and the Darran Valley Park by the river. Two variations are suggested: the shorter only tackling the gentle gradients once managed by trains.

Attractions   The Rhymney Valley Ridgeway Footpath follows a very quiet, unfenced road along the crest of Cefn-y-Brithdir. On a clear day, as you breast the ridge, the Black Mountains are straight ahead. Turning left, to the north and north-west, are the Brecon Beacons, with the main peaks in sharp relief. To the west, across the Darran Valley, is Gelligaer Common, while the remaining arc from south-west to north-east shows off numerous ridges of The Valleys. As the circle is completed, the distinctive shape of the Sugar Loaf, near Abergavenny, can be seen. A little way to the south-east is another landmark, a futuristic squashed tower—an important aircraft location beacon. Parc Cwm Darran is the site of the former Ogilvie Colliery, but it is hard to believe that this pretty valley was once a major coal producer. The park has large and small lakes and features a number of cascades. There are picnic sites around the park, but children will probably make a bee-line for the adventure playground.

The flora of Cefn-y-Brithdir is typical of the uplands of The Valleys—rough grassland competing with bracken, gorse, heather and bilberry, but brightened by foxgloves and the dainty yellow tormentil. The last 100 yards of the path up to the Ridgeway goes through an area of surprisingly dense thistles—this, too, an occasional feature of these areas. In the park, look out for the yellow monkey-flower alongside the Nant Bargod Rhymni. And can you spot the 'B' with a crown on top, between points 2 and 3?

Refreshments   At the Visitor Centre (opening Spring 1992) or picnic in the park.

61

Route 14
Parc Cwm Darran

4½ miles

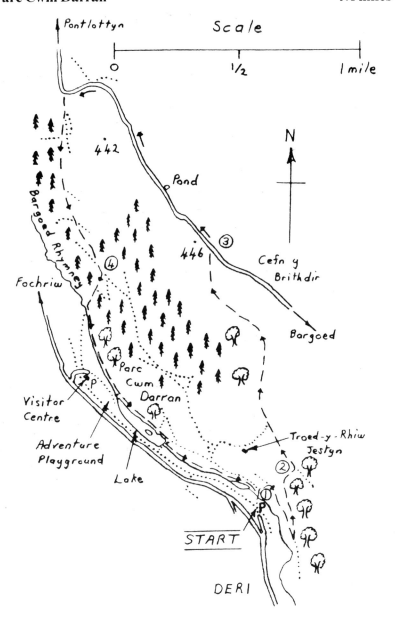

Route 14
Parc Cwm Darran

4½ miles
(shorter variations of 2 and 1½ miles)

START: *Car park at southern entrance to Parc Cwm Darran—take minor road to Deri off A469 ¼ mile north of Bargoed, then turn off Deri to Fochriw Road by Bargoed Inn (O.S. Sheet 171 G.R. 125 027).*

ROUTE:

1. *Follow the track into the Park for 50 yards then cross a stile into a field on the right. Go up the field for 50 yards then head for and cross a stile in the fence on the right. Follow the path straight on: it becomes more distinct with a fence on its left and then reaches a gate. Go through the gate and turn sharp left: the path rises just inside a wood, initially crossing the contours obliquely but, at the end of the wood, turning to go straight up to and over a stile on to a track.*

2. *Take a path to the left, just above a fence. Keep straight on as the path diverges slightly away from the fence above Troed-y-Rhiw Jestyn farm, but then re-joins the boundary. When the fenceline turns left, the path goes left across the head of a shallow valley, then swings right to reach the crest of the ridge. At the road, go left.*

3. *After a mile, the road bends to the left, then, on a sharp right hand bend, take a track to the left. Where this track splits into three, take the track on the right skirting the top edge of the forest. Where the track turns uphill as another joins it from the right, go straight ahead on a less distinct path. Cross a stile into the forest and go straight on to meet a track. Go left and, almost immediately, take a path dropping down to the right.*

4. *Cross a stile into the Park and go left immediately, keeping the river and lake on your right (unless crossing the bridge to the adventure playground at the north end of the lake). At the car park at the south end of the lake, go right then follow the east bank of the river to return to the start.*

Variation 1

Follow the track into the Park and go right on the track to Troed-y-Rhiw Jestyn. After 50 yards and a right-hand bend, take a path to the left up to and over a stile. Bear left and head up a track on the left of a line of trees to and through a gap in a high stone wall. Bear right to the nearest corner of the forest, then follow the edge of the forest to the left. Cross a stile and follow a track into the forest. A major track crosses obliquely, but keep straight on, crossing a stile to the right of a gate. Follow the track to a fork, just past some ruins: go left, dropping steeply. The gradient eases: pass a track joining from the left, then take a path which goes sharp left and down. Continue at 4.

Variation 2

Go left out of the car park then, immediately, right on the old railway track. Follow this to the adventure playground, go right, cross the river on the footbridge and go right again. Complete the walk as for the final sentence of 4.

ACCESS BY BUS

National Welsh Bustler (Service C10) passes the entrance to the park.

CASCADE ON AFON DAR

64

Route 15

3 miles
(variations of 3 and 4½ miles)

Dare Valley

Outline Dare Valley Visitor Centre — Tarren Bwllfa — Coed Morgannwg Way — Visitor Centre.

Summary This walk circles around the spectacular head of the Dare Valley, once a major coal mining centre, but now a Country Park. The outward half climbs steadily for about 700 feet, while the return follows the Coed Morgannwg Way long-distance footpath. A peregrine falcon or a ring ouzel might be seen near the crags of Tarren Bwllfa and fossils may be found in exposed shales. For the adventurous, a more strenuous variation is offered and the walk can be extended to Lluest-wen reservoir in the neighbouring valley.

Attractions On arrival, look up at the crags to the west: this height is all in the coal measures. Imagine the same level difference below your feet and you have an idea of the depth of the deep mines that once crowded this small valley. Reclamation in the early 1970s restored the Afon Dar to an open channel, creating two lakes and a cascade: tips were levelled and thousands of broadleaved trees planted, to create a country park with the emphasis on outdoor activities.

The shales of the old spoil tips are ideal for the fossil hunts organised by the Ranger Service, but petrified plants may also be spotted by the casual walker.

The initial impression is that the valley is completely closed off by a rock wall, which was probably a corrie, the source of a glacier. However, if you enjoy a challenging scramble, it is possible to follow the river up to and past the waterfall (a trickle in dry weather) to the moorland above. In this habitat, you could spot a peregrine falcon or a ring ouzel—a summer visitor, a black bird with a white breast. Alder is the predominant tree, followed by oak, birch and beech.

The Park is at the start of the 33 mile Coed Morgannwg Way path to Margam Park, near Port Talbot. On a nice day, the described route can be extended, using this path to cross the moorland to the adjacent valley of the Rhondda Fach and Lluest-wen Reservoir.

Refreshments The Visitor Centre serves light refreshments and there are picnic tables in the park.

Route 15
Dare Valley

3 miles

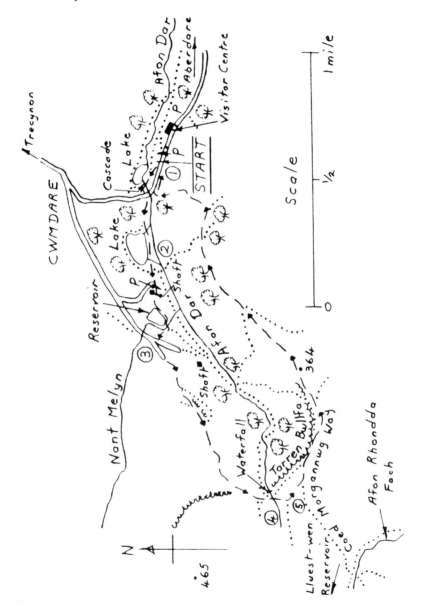

Route 15
Dare Valley
3 miles
(variations of 3 and 4½ miles)

START: *Car park west of the Visitor Centre: the Park is signed from the A465 at Hirwaun—if you approach from the south-east (off A4233), you will park on the other side of the Centre (O.S. Sheet 170 G.R. 983 027).*

ROUTE

1. *Take the path at the west end of the car park which drops down to join a main path above a lake. Go left, cross the footbridge over the cascade and continue up to a road. Head left then take a track to the right where the road bends to the left. Cross a footbridge to pass to the left of the larger lake, then cross the footbridge at the end of the lake.*

2. *Bear right across the parking area, and pass to the left of the symbolic shaft headworks to reach the reservoir fence. Go over a stile and to the left of the reservoir, leaving by the gate at the far end. Head right to emerge via a gate on to a road. Go right to a junction, then sharp left.*

3. *At the end of the road, go straight ahead on a track to the right of a house. After the house, head right, over two stiles, and up hill. Aim for a stile halfway up the fenceline ahead. Cross this, go right (steeply up hill) to join a track, then left to pass above the quarry. The path soon rises to cross a stile then swings left towards Tarren Bwllfa. Continue to the path junction by the infant Afon Dar above the waterfall.*

4. *Immediately over the river, fork right (left passes very close to the crags). At a junction by exposed rocks, go left to meet the Coed Morgannwg Way.*

5. *Go straight on. The path passes above Tarren Bwllfa then forks left before dropping gradually down the southern flank of the Dare Valley to a stile where two walls meet. Cross the stile and keep to what is now a track, curving to the right before dropping steeply to the road. Go right to return to the start.*

Variation 1 (more strenuous)

As for 1 above but, at 2, follow the Afon Dar. The path is on the right of the river for about ½ mile, then on the left for ¼ mile until a footbridge takes you back to the right side. The path now climbs 500 feet in ¼ mile and may be hard to follow. However, it climbs on to and along a prominent shoulder high on the right of the river heading for a col on the immediate right of the crags. The final section is a scramble on the right of the waterfall, then up the channel above to reach the path round the head of the valley. Turn left on this and continue at 4.

Variation 2

As for 1 to 4 above but, at 5, turn sharp right and follow the prominent stone waymark posts to, then up, the Rhondda Fach Valley to Lluest-wen reservoir. Return on the same route to 5, go right and continue as before.

ACCESS BY BUS OR TRAIN

Aberdare is well served by several bus companies and Valley Lines trains. There is a pleasant walk of a mile beside the Afon Dar from Aberdare library to the Visitor Centre. Alternatively, the Cwmdare Shamrock Shoppa bus goes to point 3 on the route.

RIDGEWAY TO PENDERYN

Route 16   5½ miles
Pontneddfechan and Penderyn

Outline   Pontneddfechan — Penderyn — Sgwd yr Eira Waterfall — Pontneddfechan.

Summary   The first 1½ miles is mainly uphill, but thereafter it is quite easy going apart from the short scramble into and out of the Hepste gorge. The route passes through open moorland, recent coniferous plantations and mature deciduous woodland, supporting a complimentary variety of plants and birds. The ridgeway to Penderyn offers wonderful views in all directions and the inspiring Sgwd yr Eira waterfall forms a spectacular river crossing behind its curtain of water.

Attractions   This is not a walk to be rushed, as there is much of interest. The first distraction may be at the car park: the old quarry is very popular with climbers and there is usually some activity on the rock faces. Just behind Craig-y-Dinas (Dinas Rock), in the gorge of the Sychryd, is a disused silica mine where the monolithic rock has been removed leaving the minimum of residual support. The silica was used to make bricks to line blast furnaces. On the opposite bank of the Sychryd, another mine, with a single main tunnel entrance and more complex internal workings, produced a limestone that polished to produce 'black marble'.

Surprisingly, this was not enough industry for this village. From the bridge over the Afon Mellte, upstream on the north bank of the river, are the remains of a gunpowder works—spread out and kept away from habitation for obvious reasons.

The ridge walk to Penderyn provides views to the south of a spectacular escarpment rising to almost 2000 feet. To the north is a panoramic skyline of peaks and ridges from the Carmarthen Fans in the west, across Fforest Fawr, to the Brecon Beacons in the east. Looking straight ahead on the track, Penderyn declares its presence with its prominent church (is that a matchstick man on its tower?) and the massive quarries beyond.

Sgwd yr Eira is formed at a fault, where a durable sandstone has been displaced vertically. Erosion of softer shales has undermined the sandstone to create a passageway behind the fall. It can be noisy and the fine mist spray may justify wearing a waterproof, but it is quite safe provided care is taken on the wet rocks. Those with the time and energy can reach three more waterfalls in the valley of the Afon Mellte by continuing beyond Sgwd yr Eira for about a mile. Trees on the steep valley sides include sessile oak, rowan, silver birch, ash and alder—the latter signalling the wettest ground

continued on page 72

Route 16
Pontneddfechan and Penderyn

5½ miles

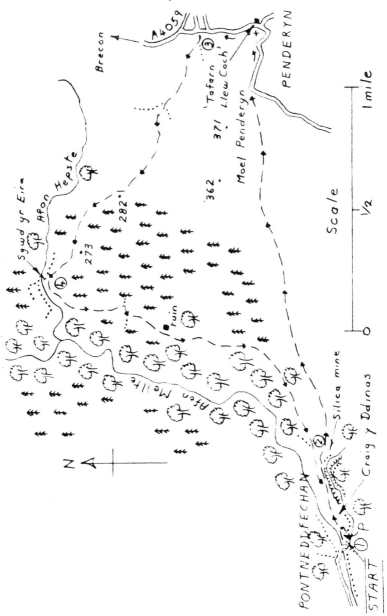

Route 16
Pontneddfechan and Penderyn   5½ miles

START: *Quarry car park at Craig y Dinas, extreme east end of Pontneddfechan—leave the A4109 at Glyn-Neath on the B4242, follow 'waterfalls' signs and go straight on by Craig y Dinas Hotel (O.S. Sheet 160 G.R. 911 079).*

ROUTE

1. *Take the path which rises steeply on the north side of Craig y Dinas and bear right at the top. The path soon follows a fence above the Sychryd gorge. Just after the fence ends, pass a path to the right leading down to the silica mine, then bear right across a shallow valley.*

2. *The path now climbs steadily for a mile up a ridge, passing through one gate before reaching its high point on Moel Penderyn, from where it drops down to emerge, via a gate, on to a road. Follow the road straight ahead, pass a road to the right near the church and continue to the second of two further roads to the right. Here, take a track to the left.*

3. *Where the track forks, bear right (the route from here to Sgwd yr Eira has yellow waymarking). Where the main track turns left, cross the stile straight ahead and follow a track on the right of the old quarries. Ignore lesser tracks diverging to right and left until some spoil heaps are reached, then go right. Follow a path curving to the right to a stile at the corner of fences. Cross the stile and go left beside a fence. Cross the next stile and head right adjacent to a fence. Where the fence turns right, take a path to the left. After 200 yards, the path bears right and drops down to some large boulders, marking the steep path and steps down to the waterfall.*

4. *After visiting Sgwd yr Eira, return to the large boulders and take the path to the right, generally following the contours around the steep valley side above the confluence of the Hepste and Mellte rivers. Go right at a T-junction of paths and, after 50 yards, take the path to the left. Just past a ruin, the path crosses a small side valley, rises slightly, then follows the contour, crossing two stiles. The path turns right and left in quick succession then swings gradually round to the right, before dropping down to a gate. After the gate, cross a stream and follow the path down to, then along a small ridge. Pass a path to the right and rejoin the outward route above the Sychryd gorge. Go right to return to the car park.*

ACCESS BY BUS
National Welsh Service X5 stops just over the bridge from the car park.

71

and once used locally to make soles for clogs. In the last mile of the walk, can you spot water mint and wild thyme?

Refreshments   Tafarn Llew Coch (Red Lion Inn) in Penderyn offers limited light snacks (but does have a reputation for real ale). About ½ mile from the car park, in Pontneddfechan, The Angel and Craig y Dinas Hotel provide a wide range of refreshments.

SGWD YR EIRA WATERFALL

APPENDIX
ROUTES IN ORDER OF DIFFICULTY

The following grading relates to a family with young children, not to seasoned adult walkers.

Easy:
Route 5 — *Forest Farm (variation), 2 miles*
Route 3 — *Ogmore and Merthyr Mawr (variation), 1½ miles*
Route 14 — *Parc Cwm Darran (variation 2), 1½ miles*
Route 5 — *Forest Farm, 3 miles*
Route 1 — *Cosmeston and Lavernock, 3½ miles*
Route 3 — *Ogmore and Merthyr Mawr, 3 miles*
Route 9 — *Llantrisant (variations), 1½ and 2 miles*
Route 2 — *Llantwit Major, 3½ miles*

Moderate:
Route 7 — *Rudry (variation 1), 3 miles*
Route 14 — *Parc Cwm Darran (variation 1), 2 miles*
Route 12 — *Llanwonno (variation), 2 miles*
Route 6 — *Machen and Draethen (variation), 3 miles*
Route 2 — *Llantwit Major (linear variation), 5½ miles*
Route 4 — *Cowbridge, Llansannor and Graig Penllyn (variation 2), 4 miles*
Route 9 — *Llantrisant, 3 miles*
Route 13 — *Quaker's Yard, 4 miles*
Route 15 — *Dare Valley, 3 miles*
Route 6 — *Machen and Draethen, 4½ miles*
Route 8 — *Gwaelod-y-Garth (variation), 3½ miles*
Route 15 — *Dare Valley (variation 1), 3 miles*
Route 10 — *Pont Rhyd-y-Cyff (variation), 3½ miles*
Route 11 — *Llwynypia Mountain (variation), 2½ miles*
Route 4 — *Cowbridge, Llansannor and Graig Penllyn (variation 1), 5½ miles*
Route 12 — *Llanwonno, 4 miles*

More Strenuous:
Route 7 — *Rudry (variation 2), 4½ miles*
Route 15 — *Dare Valley (variation 2), 4½ miles*
Route 4 — *Cowbridge, Llansannor and Graig Penllyn, 6 miles*
Route 8 — *Gwaelod-y-Garth, 4½ miles*
Route 14 — *Parc Cwm Darran, 4½ miles*
Route 11 — *Llwynypia Mountain, 4 miles*
Route 7 — *Rudry, 5½ miles*
Route 10 — *Pont Rhyd-y-Cyff, 5½ miles*
Route 16 — *Pontneddfechan and Penderyn, 5½ miles*

PUBLIC TRANSPORT

British Rail ....Cardiff 228000
Cardiff Bus ....Cardiff 396521
Cynon Valley Transport Ltd ....Aberdare 881888
Islwyn Borough Transport Ltd ....Blackwood 226622
National Welsh Ltd...Aberdare 872361
                                            Barry 733236
                                            Bridgend 662626
                                            Caerphilly 867003
                                            Cardiff 371331
                                            Merthyr 4728
                                            Pontypridd 485460
                                            Porth 682671
Shamrock Shoppa ....Pontypridd 404477

PLACES OF INTEREST

Just in case it rains . . . the following are partly or completely under cover and should be of interest to the whole family.

Barry Island Pleasure Park—all the fun of the fair—0446 741250

Brecon Mountain Railway, Pant, Merthyr Tydfil—narrow gauge trains into the Brecon Beacons—0685 4854

Caerphilly Castle—with the tower that out-leans that at Pisa—0222 883143

Cambrian Lampworks, Robertstown, Aberdare—magic world of the miner's lamp (phone first)—0685 876107

Cardiff Castle—dating from Roman times, but restored and elaborated upon in the 19th century—0222 822083

Castell Coch, Tongwynlais, Cardiff—extravagantly rebuilt, picture-book castle—0222 810101

Coney Beach, Porthcawl—amusement park—0656 788911

Cosmeston Medieval Village, near Penarth—reconstructed 14th century village—0222 708686

Cyfartha Castle Museum, Merthyr Tydfil—former ironmaster's home displaying the social and industrial history of the town—0685 723112

Ewenny Pottery—see the potter at work—0656 653020

Llancaiach Fawr, near Nelson—history brought to life: a journey back to the Civil War—0443 412248

Llanerch Vineyard, Hensol, Pendoylan—home of Cariad Wines—0443 225877

Marlborough Military Models, The Duchy, Panty Gog, Pontycymmer—see lead soldiers crafted—0656 871774

Model House Craft & Design Centre, Bull Ring, Llantrisant—money making exhibition and craftsmen at work—0443 237758

National Museum of Wales, Cathays Park, Cardiff—progressive and lively, fully deserving its 'national' title—0222 397951

Pontypridd Historical Centre, Bridge Street, Pontypridd—museum of local history and culture—0443 402077

Rhondda Heritage Park, Trehafod, Rhondda—'Black Gold, the story of coal'—0443 682036

Stuart Crystal Glassworks, Aberbargoed—hand produced fine crystal manufacture—0443 820044

Techniquest, Bute Street, Cardiff—hands on exhibition of science and technology—0222 460211

Wales Aircraft Museum, Cardiff-Wales Airport, Rhoose—display of aircraft and helicopters—0446 710135

Welsh Folk Museum, St. Fagans, Cardiff—buildings from all over Wales, preserved in the grounds of a castle, plus craft demonstrations—0222 569441
Welsh Hawking Centre, Weycock Road, Barry—birds of prey put through their paces most days—0446 734687
Welsh Industrial and Maritime Museum, Bute Street, Cardiff—exhibits of industry and transport in Wales, many of special appeal to inquisitive children—0222 481919
Ynysfach Engine House, Merthyr Tydfil—the story of iron—0685 721858

INFORMATION OFFICES
Barry, The Promenade—0446 747171
Cardiff, 8–14 Bridge Street—0222 227281
Caerphilly, Park Lane—0222 851378
Cowbridge, 79 Eastgate—0446 772073
Llantwit Major, Town Hall—0446 796086
Merthyr Tydfil, 14a Glebeland Street—0685 79884
Penarth, Stanwell Road—0222 706223
Porthcawl, John Street—0656 712211
Pontneddfechan—0639 721795
Pontypridd, Bridge Street—0443 402077
Sarn, Service Area, M4 junction 36—0656 654906

SILICA MINE, SYCHRYD GORGE

SOME WELSH WORDS OF GEOGRAPHICAL SIGNIFICANCE

Aber—mouth (of river)
Afon—river
Bach (or fach)—small, little
Blaen—point, tip
Bryn—hill
Bwlch—gap, pass
Caer (or gaer)—fort
Capel—chapel
Carreg—stone
Castell—castle
Cefn—back, ridge
Coch—red
Coed—wood, trees
Croes (or groes)—cross
Cwm—valley
Cyhoeddus—public
Eglwys—church
Ffynnon—well, spring
Graig (or craig)—rock
Gwaelod—bottom
Heol—street, road
Isaf—lowest
Llan—enclosure: but, commonly, church
Llwybr—footpath
Llwyn—grove, bush
Llyn—lake
Maen (or faen)—stone
Mawr (or fawr)—big, large
Melin (or felin)—mill
Moel (or foel)—bare hill
Mynydd—mountain
Nant—brook, stream
Neuadd—hall
Newydd—new
Pant—hollow, valley
Parc—park
Pont—bridge
Rhaeadr—waterfall
Rhiw—hill
Rhyd—ford
Sant—saint
Sgwd—waterfall
Tafarn—inn
Tarren—knoll, rock
Traeth—beach
Troed—foot
Ty—house
Uchaf—highest
Y (or yr)—the
Ynys—island, meadow
Ysbyty—hospital
Ysgol—school
Ystrad—vale

WATERFALL ON NANT Y GWIDDON (Route 11)

FAMILY WALKS SERIES

Family Walks in the North Yorkshire Dales. Howard Beck. ISBN 0 907758 52 5.

Family Walks in West Yorkshire. Howard Beck. ISBN 0 907758 43 6.

Family Walks in Three Peaks and Malham. Howard Beck. ISBN 0 907758 42 8.

Family Walks in South Yorkshire. Norman Taylor. ISBN 0 907758 25 8.

Family Walks in the North Wales Borderlands. Gordon Emery. ISBN 0 907758 50 9.

Family Walks in Cheshire. Chris Buckland. ISBN 0 907758 29 0.

Family Walks in the Staffordshire Peak and Potteries. Les Lumsdon. ISBN 0 907758 34 7.

Family Walks in the White Peak. Norman Taylor. ISBN 0 907758 09 6.

Family Walks in the Dark Peak. Norman Taylor. ISBN 0 907758 16 9.

Family Walks in Snowdonia. Laurence Main. ISBN 0 907758 32 0.

Family Walks in Mid Wales. Laurence Main. ISBN 0 907758 27 4.

Family Walks in South Shropshire. Marian Newton. ISBN 0 907758 30 4.

Family Walks in the Teme Valley. Camilla Harrison. ISBN 0 907758 45 2.

Family Walks in Hereford and Worcester. Gordon Ottewell. ISBN 0 907758 20 7.

Family Walks around Cardiff and the Valleys. Gordon Hindess. ISBN 0 907758 54 1.

Family Walks in the Wye Valley. Heather and Jon Hurley. ISBN 0 907758 26 6.

Family Walks in Warwickshire. Geoff Allen. ISBN 0 907758 53 3.

Family Walks around Stratford and Banbury. Gordon Ottewell. ISBN 0 907758 49 5.

Family Walks in the Cotswolds. Gordon Ottewell. ISBN 0 907758 15 0.

Family Walks in South Gloucestershire. Gordon Ottewell. ISBN 0 907758 33 9.

Family Walks in Oxfordshire. Laurence Main. ISBN 0 907758 38 X.

Family Walks around Bristol, Bath and the Mendips. Nigel Vile. ISBN 0 907758 19 3.

Family Walks in Wiltshire. Nigel Vile. ISBN 0 907758 21 5.

Family Walks in Berkshire and North Hampshire. Kathy Sharp. ISBN 0 907758 37 1.

Family Walks on Exmoor and the Quantocks. John Caswell. ISBN 0 907758 46 0.

Family Walks in Mendip, Avalon and Sedgemoor. Nigel Vile. ISBN 0 907758 41 X.

Family Walks in Cornwall. John Caswell. ISBN 0 907758 55 X.

Family Walks on the Isle of Wight. Laurence Main. ISBN 0 907758 56 8.

Family Walks in North West Kent. Clive Cutter. ISBN 0 907758 36 3.

Family Walks in the Weald of Kent and Sussex. Clive and Sally Cutter. ISBN 0 907758 51 7.

- -

The Publishers, D. J. Mitchell and E. G. Power welcome suggestions for further titles in this Series; and will be pleased to consider manuscripts relating to Derbyshire from new or established authors.

- -